HOLIDAYS
AND
TRADITIONS

Kyla Steinkraus

Rourke
Educational Media

rourkeeducationalmedia.com

Weird, True Traditions and Where to Find Them.

1. **Canada** The International Hair Freezing Contest
2. **Korea** Hangeul Proclamation Day
3. **Mexico** Día de Muertos, Night of the Radishes, Twelve Grapes
4. **Italy** 1194 revolt
5. **Spain** La Tomatina, Tió de Nadal, Running of the Bulls
6. **Japan** KFC Christmas
7. **Ukraine** A Spidery Christmas
8. **Germany** World Competitive Christmas Tree Throwing Championship
9. **Ecuador** Suitcase Around the Block
10. **Romania** New Year's Eve tradition of wearing bear costumes and furs
11. **Denmark** New Year's Eve tradition of smashing plates
12. **Thailand** Monkey Buffet Festival
13. **Turkenistan** National Melon Day
14. **England** International Worm Charming Festival
15. **United States of America** Wisconsin State Cow Chip Throw and Festival, Gilroy Garlic Festival, Punkin Chunkin, Avon Heritage Duct Tape Festival, Lower Keys Underwater Music Festival

Table of Contents

Wacky and Wonderful

Celebrations are fun. And strange celebrations can be even more fun. How does a giant food fight sound? Or perhaps a hair-freezing contest! Every **culture** has its own traditions, **customs**, and festivals, but some are a bit more unusual than others. From creative twists on traditional holidays to unique **regional** celebrations, you can find something wacky and wonderful on every continent.

A Hair-Raising Tradition

There's a cool competition each year in Whitehorse, Yukon, Canada: The International Hair Freezing Contest. Participants use nothing but water and the frigid air to create wild styles. With temperatures well below zero, it only takes a few minutes for hair to freeze!

Honoring the Alphabet

Koreans use their own unique alphabet called Hangeul.
Before it was created, only wealthy, upper-class Koreans
could read and write, using complicated Chinese characters.
Average Koreans didn't have the time or money to learn this
writing system. The invention of Hangeul changed everything
by giving ordinary citizens an easy way to read and write.
Each year on October 9, South Koreans celebrate Hangeul
Proclamation Day. North Korea celebrates on January 15.

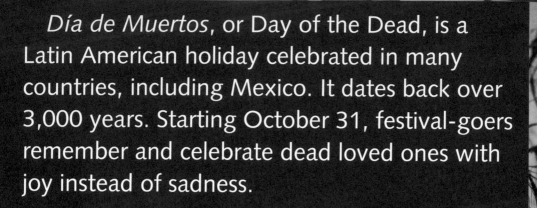

Día de Muertos, or Day of the Dead, is a Latin American holiday celebrated in many countries, including Mexico. It dates back over 3,000 years. Starting October 31, festival-goers remember and celebrate dead loved ones with joy instead of sadness.

Celebrating the Dead
Skulls are a symbol of this holiday—including chocolate and sugar skulls, skull cookies, cupcakes, and sweet bread with skull-shaped frosting. People also wear skull masks or paint skulls on their faces.

People light candles and leave presents on friends' and relatives' graves. There are parades and dancing. Participants wear bright colors and beautiful costumes.

Every February, people in Ivrea, Italy, form teams to recreate an event that happened more than 800 years ago: the 1194 revolt against the country's king. They don't use weapons, though. Instead, they throw oranges. It's a giant food fight!

In Buñol, Spain, tens of thousands of people gather on the last Wednesday of August for La Tomatina. The small town's population of 9,000 triples as visitors come to throw more than 220,000 pounds (99,790 kilograms) of overripe tomatoes in the streets.

La Tomatina begins with someone climbing a tall, greased pole to reach a ham placed at the top. This is tricky and can take a while. Water cannons are fired to signal the start of the battle. Everyone is covered head to toe in red tomato paste! One hour of tomato-tossing chaos later, the clean-up begins.

Christmas Around the World

Which holiday is celebrated with spider webs, radishes, and buckets of fried chicken? You might be surprised. It's Christmas!

In Japan, traditional Christmas dinner isn't turkey or ham with gravy, it's a bucket of Kentucky Fried Chicken's famous meal! Every Christmas, millions of people line up outside KFC restaurants around the country.

The Power of Advertising

The KFC Christmas dinner is the result of a 1970s marketing campaign. At the time, there was no traditional Christmas celebration in Japan. Takeshi Okawara, the manager of Japan's first KFC, came up with the idea to market "party barrels" of chicken for the holidays after overhearing foreigners say they missed having turkey for Christmas.

KFC's Christmas meal is served in festive holiday buckets. The tradition is so popular, KFC recommends reserving your Christmas meal months in advance!

Christmas trees in the Ukraine aren't decorated with candy canes and twinkling lights. They are decorated with spider webs for good luck! The webs aren't from real spiders, of course. They are made with crystal, paper, metal, or plastic.

A Spidery Christmas
The spider web tradition comes from the **legend** of a poor family with no money to decorate their tree. When the children woke up Christmas morning, spiders had spun webs of silk in the branches. The rising sun caused the webs to sparkle like lights and tinsel.

In Oaxaca, Mexico, children spend Christmas Eve partying with radishes. The Night of the Radishes, or *Noche De Ràbanos*, is a festival with parades, dances, and a radish sculpture competition.

Experts sculpt and carve the red root vegetable into faces, flags, animals, and nativity scenes. The festival is so popular, the city bought a farm just to grow radishes.

The Night of the Radishes festival was established in 1897.

The *Tió de Nadal*, or Christmas log, in the Catalan region in Spain is a hollow log that stands on stick legs. The log has a painted face on one end and wears a red hat. A few weeks before Christmas, kids give the log nuts and fruit to eat and keep it warm with a small blanket. On Christmas Day, they hit the log with sticks and sing it a song. Presents appear beneath the blanket under the log. The Tió de Nadal log "poops" them out!

It's usually no fun to throw out the Christmas tree after the holidays are over. But in Weidenburg, Germany, people can't wait to toss their trees.

The town hosts the World Competitive Christmas Tree Throwing Championship. Participants shot-put, javelin toss, or pole-vault their trees to compete in the championship.

Ringing in the New Year

The New Year is the world's most celebrated holiday. But it wasn't always on the first of January.

The earliest recorded New Year festivities date back 4,000 years ago. Ancient Babylonians celebrated the first new moon following the **vernal** equinox, or the day in late March with an equal amount of sunlight and darkness. The celebration lasted 11 days, with a different ritual for each day.

The Babylonian New Year's festival **honored** the supreme god Marduk, his crown prince Nabû, and other gods.

These days, people around the world ring in the New Year in some wild ways! In Ecuador, people walk around their neighborhoods with empty suitcases. This is supposed to bring them more travel opportunities in the coming year.

In Romania, people dress up in bear costumes and furs, then dance from house to house to ward off evil.

In Denmark, people smash plates against their friends' doors to celebrate the New Year. The broken china is supposed to bring good luck. The bigger the pile of smashed plates, the better! They also jump off a chair at midnight. Taking your feet off the ground at midnight is supposed to leave behind bad spirits as you jump into a fresh year.

Your Underwear Is Showing!
In Venezuela, people wear bright yellow underwear on New Year's Eve for good luck. Sometimes they wear them outside their clothes, for all to see.

In Mexico, people eat 12 grapes on New Year's Eve, one for each of the 12 chimes of the clock at midnight and the months of the year. A wish is made on each grape. Beware the sour grapes! If you get one, that month is thought to be unlucky.

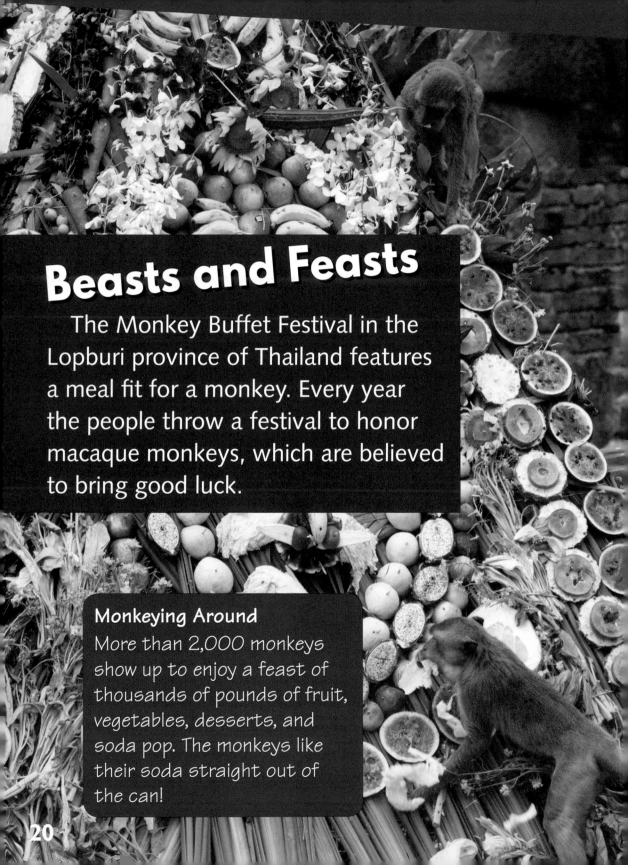

Beasts and Feasts

The Monkey Buffet Festival in the Lopburi province of Thailand features a meal fit for a monkey. Every year the people throw a festival to honor macaque monkeys, which are believed to bring good luck.

Monkeying Around

More than 2,000 monkeys show up to enjoy a feast of thousands of pounds of fruit, vegetables, desserts, and soda pop. The monkeys like their soda straight out of the can!

Imagine being chased by a horned beast. Does that sound like fun? Some people think so. At the San Fermin Festival, six bulls chase brave volunteers through the streets in Pamplona, Spain.

The Running of the Bulls traces back to 1591, when it became tradition to run the bulls to the bullfighting ring. Bull runners are called *mozos*. Mozos traditionally wear all white with a red sash or belt.

Weird American Traditions and Festivals

Each year for Thanksgiving, the U.S. president is presented with a turkey at a special ceremony. From 1940 until 1989, the president could choose whether to pardon the turkey. Sometimes it ended up as dinner, sometimes it was sent back to live on the farm. In 1989, George H.W. Bush declared the pardon a permanent part of the event, so all the turkeys presented to presidents are guaranteed a pardon!

Speaking of farm animals, the Wisconsin State Cow Chip Throw and Festival sounds fun—until you realize that a cow chip is a dried piece of cow poop! Located in  the town of Prairie de Sac, the festival includes a parade, crafts and food, and of course, the cow-chip-throwing competition. The current record stands at 248 feet (75.6 meters).

Gilroy, California, is home to one of the largest—and possibly strongest smelling—food festivals in the U.S.: the Gilroy Garlic Festival. The celebration features all things garlic, from garlic braiding to garlic ice cream.

GARLIC·ICE·CREAM

Featuring

GARLIC VANILLA   GARLIC CHOCOLATE
GARLIC PISTACHIO   GARLIC PECAN PRALINE
GARLIC SNICKERDOODLE

PLAIN VANILLA & PLAIN BURGUNDY CHERRY

Delaware hosts the country's first and largest pumpkin tossing contest. During Punkin Chunkin, people use catapults, air cannons, and other tools to make their pumpkins fly. The record is 4,694 feet (1.4 kilometers).

Fabulous Food
Americans celebrate their favorite foods with *National Pizza Day* on February 9, *National French Fries Day* on June 13, and *National Ice Cream Day* on the third Sunday in July.

The Avon Heritage Duct Tape Festival in Avon, Ohio, is all about—you guessed it!—duct tape. The celebration includes duct tape sculptures, fashions, and of course, a parade!

The Lower Keys Underwater Music Festival has been jamming in the Florida Keys for more than 30 years. Music is piped underwater with speakers suspended under boats. Divers can check out the marine life and coral reefs, and may just find a mermaid playing a starfish guitar.

With so many fascinating cultures, holidays, festivals, and traditions around the world, there's something to celebrate every day!

Need more reasons to celebrate? How about:

Peculiar People Day, January 10

National Rubber Duckie Day, January 13

National Dress Up Your Pet Day, January 14

National Nothing Day, January 16

National Opposite Day, January 25

No Socks Day, May 8

Lost Sock Memorial Day, May 9

Take Your Pants for a Walk Day, July 27

More...Really Weird, True Facts!

Chinese New Year's Day is the first day of the Chinese lunar calendar. The date is different each year, but is always between January 21 and February 20. As part of the celebration, Chinese bosses, leaders, and elders give their counterparts red envelopes with cash in them. Billions of red envelopes are exchanged!

About 400 of the world's 1,600 melon varieties have historical links to Turkmenistan, so it's only natural to have a national Melon Day! To celebrate, markets and fairs have melon tastings and melon-related competitions all over the country.

Ever tried to charm a worm? The village of Blackawton, England, hosts the International Worm Charming Festival every year. Competitors of all ages try whatever they can think of to get the worms out of the ground—except digging! The festivities begin with a "worm up," then charmers have 15 minutes to get the most worms.

Valentine's Day is one of the most celebrated holidays worldwide. It is the second most popular card-giving holiday, right after Christmas!
Americans exchange more than 1.6 billion Christmas greeting cards. They exchange about 150 million for Valentine's Day.

Crystal Falls, Michigan is home to one of the world's largest living organisms, a fungus that sprawls over 48 acres (19.42 hectares). Naturally, it's also home to the Humongous Fungus Fest, which lasts three days and includes the world's largest mushroom pizza.

In Norway, people hide all their brooms on Christmas Eve. According to legend, that's when witches come out.

Cheese rolling is a tradition in Gloucester in England. At the Cooper's Hill Cheese-Rolling and Wake, a heavy round of Double Gloucester cheese gets a head start down the steep hill before the runners chase after it. The first person to cross the finish line at the bottom of the hill wins the cheese.

Index

Glossary

culture (KUHL-chur): the ideas, customs, traditions, and way of life of a group of people

customs (KUHSS-tuhms): traditions in a culture or society

legend (LEJ-uhnd): a story handed down from earlier times

honored (ON-ur-ed): good, deserving of praise and privilege

regional (REE-juhn-uhl): relating to or characteristic of a region

vernal (VER-nuhl): of, in, or relating to spring

Show What You Know

1. How did the KFC Christmas tradition begin in Japan?

2. How long have people been celebrating the New Year?

3. What does the Tió de Nadal do on Christmas Day?

4. How many grapes do people in Mexico eat on New Year's Eve?

5. What do bull runners usually wear?

Websites to Visit

www.brownielocks.com/contents.html#Traditions

www.simplykinder.com/christmas-around-world-videos-kids

www.timeforkids.com/news/holidays-are-here/11516

About the Author

Kyla Steinkraus lives in Atlanta, GA with her family and two spoiled cats. She loves to read, draw, travel, and eat dark chocolate. A really weird, totally true fact about Kyla is that she sometimes thinks aloud. She's been known to argue with herself!

Meet The Author!
www.meetREMauthors.com

www.rourkeeducationalmedia.com

PHOTO CREDITS: Cover and title page: ©mtreasure, ©osorioartisl, ©ajt, ©agcuesta, ©ell2550, ©JackF; table of contents: ©catinsyrup; p.4: ©Anton Watman; p.5: ©NoonBuSin; p.6: ©agcuesta; p.7: ©mofles; p.8: ©AGaeta, ©RiccardoChiades; p.9, 21: ©mmeee; p.10: ©malerapaso; p.11: ©Fike2308 | Dreamstime.com; p.12: ©Louise Wightman; p.13: ©bajinda, ©Jennifer Booher/Alamy Stock Photo; p.14: ©Natursports; p.15: ©Josie Desmarais; p.16: ©Andrea Izzotti; p.17: ©Sherwin McGehee, ©Kristen Soper/Alamy Stock Photo; p.18: ©Eduardo Jose Bernardino; p.19: ©kiko_jimenez; p.20: ©Manit Larpluecha; p.23: ©George Bush Presidential Library and Museum/NARA; p.23: ©SanerG, ©DanielPrudek; p.24: ©Mariusz S. Jurgielewicz; p.25: ©David McGlynn/Alamy Stock Photo, ©Aleksandor Zoric; p.26: ©Jules_Kitano, ©Carlien Beukes; p.27: ©sofiaworld; p.28: ©sunstock, ©Coprid; p.29: ©Joe Biafore, ©1000 Words

Edited by: Keli Sipperley
Cover design by: Tara Raymo
Interior design by: Rhea Magaro-Wallace

Library of Congress PCN Data

Holidays and Traditions / Kyla Steinkraus
(Weird, True Facts)
ISBN 978-1-68342-370-6 (hard cover)
ISBN 978-1-68342-536-6 (e-Book)
Library of Congress Control Number: 2017931262

Rourke Educational Media
Printed in the United States of America,
North Mankato, Minnesota